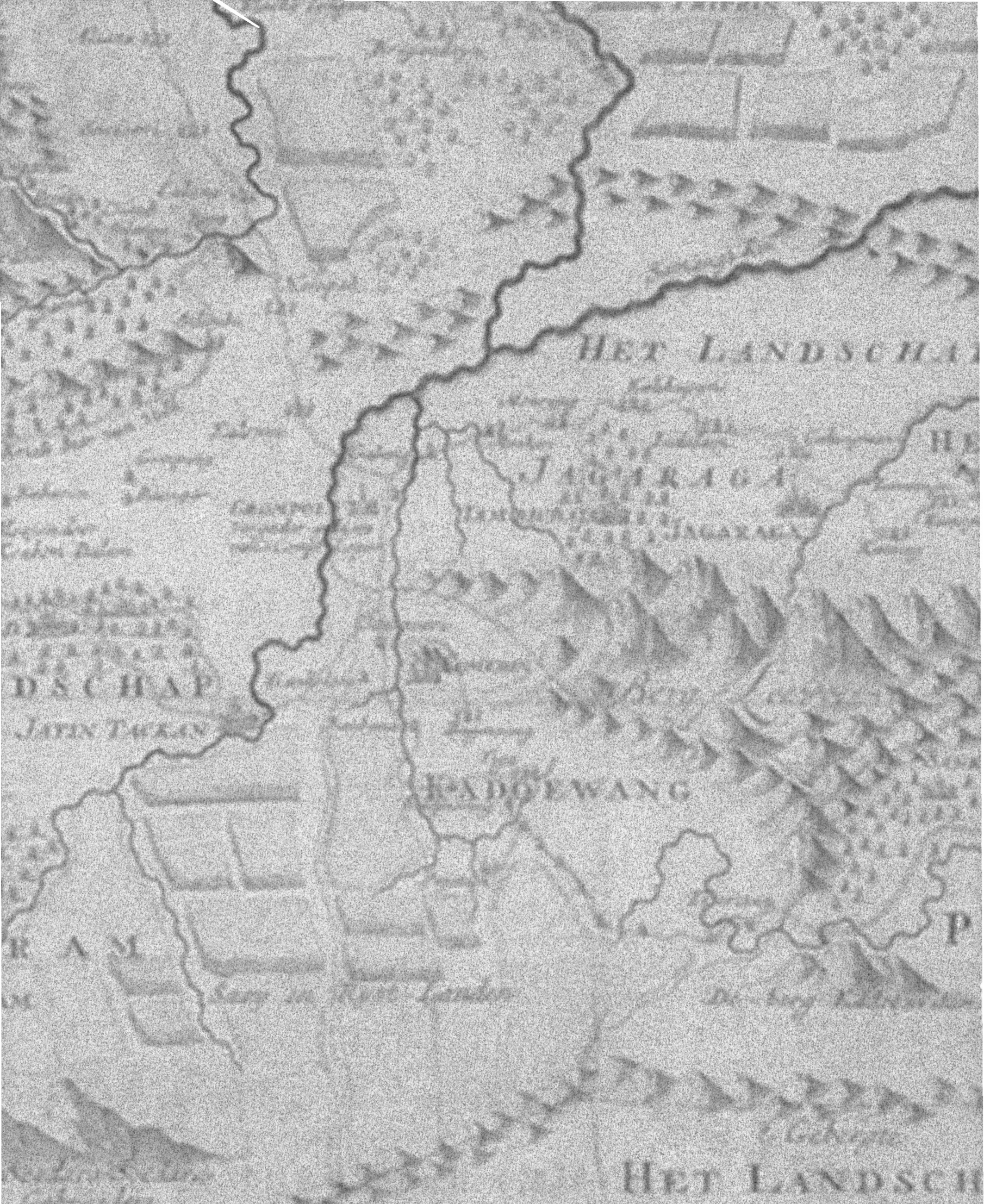

TRACES OF SUGAR

TRACES OF SUGAR
THE LEGACY OF JAVA'S SUGAR INDUSTRY

KRISNINA MAHARANI A. TANDJUNG

WWI
Foundation

Yayasan Warna Warni Indonesia

TRACES OF SUGAR

THE LEGACY OF JAVA'S SUGAR INDUSTRY

© 2010 Krisnina Maharani A. Tandjung

Author
Krisnina Maharani A. Tandjung

Research and Documentation
Rachmad Bahari

Translator
Kabar Media

Graphic Designer
Johannes Satyadi

Photographer
WB Photography
(Ibham Jasin, Fiqih, Mohammad Ramadan)

Publisher
Yayasan Warna Warni Indonesia
Jalan Purnawarman No. 18 Kebayoran Baru
Jakarta 12110
Telp (62-21) 724 7318   Faks (62-21) 726 2519
Website : www.warnawarniindonesia.org
Email : info@warnawarniindonesia.org

Printer
PT. Jayakarta Agung Offset

First Edition 2010

ISBN 978-979-1383-08-0

TABLE OF CONTENTS

FOREWORD

I am truly grateful that I could finally complete this book, **TRACES OF SUGAR**. It has long been my desire to make it happen, so that we can be grateful to be a nation that is blessed by God with natural wealth that is *gemah ripah loh jinawi*, like an emerald in the Equator, or as Westerners also often dub it, *green gold*. I wrote this book because I believe that there is still much cultural history of our nation that we have not yet discovered, and that has not received attention, such as the background of the plantation life, because the sugar cane industry in Java has very close links with the process of cultural assimilation from all national roots. Therefore, I think this book is interesting and important, not only for the public who do not know about life on plantations, but also for the plantation community itself. I hope that this book will help you to build awareness of the cultural richness of the Indonesian nation.

I would like to invite readers to learn about plantations, the history of which is very significant in the building of the civilization and culture of Indonesia. One of its legacies can be seen in buildings and works of architecture. A building or a piece of architecture can portray the phenomenon of a civilization at a certain time in history.

This book invites readers to revisit memories of the old Dutch era, an era in which there was *tanam paksa* ('compulsory planting' or *cultuurstelsel*: a Dutch government policy in the mid-nineteenth century that required a portion of agricultural production to be devoted to export crops), and its impact, namely the growth of private sector contribution in building the sugar industry. This is what you can enjoy in this book: a story about the footprint of sugar, and the heritage of the sugar industry.

This essay covers the history of entrepreneurship in sugar before the arrival of the VOC up to the creation of the 'sugar town' of *Oosthoek*/Pasuruan, and the centre of sugar (Surabaya). Although there are many photos of beautiful historic buildings, this book is not about the study of architecture. These photographs tell stories of the cultural background of the beautiful buildings.

As the main theme, I chose East Java, because this region has been the centre of the sugar industry since the beginning, and is known by the locals as an area that is *emas hijau* ('green gold' – a fertile and rich region). Until now, East Java is still the country's largest sugar supplier at the national level.

Cultivation of cane sugar grew rapidly into a sugar industry in the colonial era, and therefore this book is not detached from the presence of the Dutch – from its arrival to the many elements of its cultural heritage. The relationship between the Dutch and the kings of Java (Mataram) has opened our eyes about Dutch imperialism in the land of Java, and the story of fighting imperialism through the Diponegoro War or the Java War (1825-1830). War had drained Dutch government resources to the extent that it almost went bankrupt.

After the Diponegoro War, the Dutch actually strengthened their power not only in Java, but also across the whole archipelago, by imposing new regulations of enforced cultivation as 'compensation for war costs'. This era of *tanam paksa* ended when the Dutch government came up with new policies that liberalized the economy and the agrarian system in the colony, and had an impact on the increased building of economic infrastructure, and with the movement towards modern principles in Java. Various facilities were built, embodied with various architectural styles in those cities at the centre of economic activity. Java also became an international model for the cultivation of sugarcane.

The story of the liberal economic activities of the colonial era can be found in Chapter I, THE ECHO OF SUGAR. In addition we also show works of art or stories from the political movement against *tanam paksa*

through such characters as Multatuli, Van Deventer, and Baron van Hoevel. **The history of sugar has cultural resonance in the colonies and it became part of the establishment of Indonesian nationality.**

In Chapter II, THE MARCH OF SUGAR, I present the dynamics of employment, the condition of the sugar factories, and the current conditions of the sugar cane plantations (2009). The expanse of the sugar cane area and the stories of the workers on the plantation are meant to invite readers to better comprehend life in the plantations and sugar factories. The sugar factories that we have now are mostly a legacy of the colonial era. British-owned sugar factories from the colonial period are still visited by descendants of the owners from Britain. Those old machines that are still producing have, along with the other facilities, become part of the intricate systems of the current sugar industry.

In Chapter III, SUGAR TOWN, I would like to invite you to open your eyes to the wonderful legacy on the eastern tip of Java, or *Oosthoek*. The beautiful buildings scattered around the town of Pasuruan are evidence of the past prosperity of this city, which used to be called the *Pasar Uang* (money market). In the past, there were many industries that were started here. The charming architecture of the Tionghoa (Chinese Indonesian) family, who were known as 'Javanese royalty', is part of a mosaic of Indonesian culture that originated in Java.

The journey of sugar in this book ends in Surabaya. Java's position as 'the land of sugar cane' can be witnessed in the HVA (Handelsvereeniging Amsterdam), the largest private plantation office building, which is now used as the building of PTPN XI (*Perseroan Terbatas Perkebunan Negara* – the holding

company for state-owned plantations). This majestic structure was built by architects and engineers from the firm of Hulswit, Fermont, Ed. Cuypers in 1921 and became the pride of the city of Surabaya at that time. The architecture of a building always emphasizes the variety of character of the local society. Various corners of the building and a little history of the city of Surabaya is recorded in Chapter IV, as a CENTER OF SUGAR, which I have used as the title of the chapter.

While thanking God Almighty, I also thank the Government of the Republic of Indonesia through the Ministry of Culture and Tourism, Ministry of Commerce, and the Governor of East Java, Dr. H. Soekarwo. Sincere gratitude to PT Bank Mandiri (Persero) Tbk, PT Maspion Group, PT Bank Rakyat Indonesia (Persero) Tbk, PT Bank Bukopin, Asosiasi Gula Rafinasi Indonesia, PT Jamsostek (Persero), PT Rajawali Nusantara Indonesia (Persero). To our fellow cultural enthusiasts, Bapak KPA Wiwoho Basuki Tjokrohadiningrat, Ibu Lies Yusgiantoro, Ibu Ike Nirwan Bakrie.

Endless gratitude is also addressed to Bapak Drs. Irwan Basri, MM, President Director of PTPN XI (Persero) and all staff that have facilitated our work. Our thanks are addressed also to all the directors of PTPN IX (Persero) and PTPN X (Persero) for allowing us to photograph.

To the owners of the houses in Pasuruan, namely: the family of Bapak Fachir Muhammad Thalib, the family of Ibu Kwee Norma Wardhana Zecha, and the family of Ibu Beatricia Sulistyani Handayani Dwiningsih, who opened their hearts to give us permission to photograph their homes. Without their permission it would have been impossible to make this book as beautiful as it is.

We also thank to Bapak Puji Harsono, numismatist (collector of historical currency) for his willingness to lend historic coins and maps to be photographed as illustrations for this book.

Thanks to Mr Roger Tol, the head of the Koninklijk Instituut voor Taal, Land en Volkenkunde (KITLV) Jakarta, for his assistance with providing old photographs from the Leiden KITLV collection in digital format so that they could be presented well in this book. Thanks are also due to the Indonesian Ambassador to the Kingdom of the Netherlands, H.E. Junus Effendi Habibie. Thanks also to Mr. James de Rave of Kedaung Group, Yori Antar, architect and photographer, Nadia and Ria, Architecture Data Center in Jakarta, and to Atmaja Tjiptobiantoro.

Thanks to the WB Photography team (Ibham Jasin, et al.) and to my colleagues at the Warna Warni Indonesia Foundation: Rachmad Bahari as research associate, and Agustian Budi Prasetya as proofreader, and the ladies that have strived to get this book published: Efin Soehada, Terry Wijaya Supit, Liza Hariara Tambunan, Yessi Haryanda, Sianny Farich, Dewi Triman Muhklis, and Ahmad Baedillah and Denny Prasetyaningsih who faithfully and patiently helped typing.

To friends who sincerely and happily helped me in Jakarta, Surabaya, and Pasuruan, I also wish to sincerely thank you.

Finally, thanks and gratitude for the sense of love and affection from my husband and my kids that always makes me so happy. *I Love You.*
May God bless our efforts together.

Krisnina Maharani A. Tandjung

THE ECHO OF SUGAR

*S*ugar has a lot of interesting aspects, which have not been widely studied and are thus not common knowledge.

Sugar and/or sugar cane was not only intertwined with the beginning of modern civilization in the colonial era of Java, but was also closely associated with the roots of nationhood. The cultivation of sugarcane and the sugar industry itself have influenced cultural assimilation among the multi-ethnic population of Java. Links were forged between the cultures of Java, China, and Europe (the Netherlands). From sugar, we can track and trace the process through which Indonesia became a nation.

Sugar! Its echo is indeed widespread in the formation of the history of modern Indonesia. It was initially a side commodity traded by the Dutch, as the Europeans who made expeditions to the East were mainly on a quest for spices, which had previously been transported along the thoroughfare known as the Silk Road. Then, sugar became a more profitable commodity than spice. The Dutch then tried to control the sugar trade. When they came to Indonesia in the late 16th century, sugar was a commodity traditionally harvested by the Tionghoa (Chinese Indonesian) people around Batavia.

The skills required to process sugar cane were brought to Java by Chinese immigrants in the 15th century. The business of making sugar started to spread in the mid-seventeenth century, south of Batavia (*ommelanden*). According to various historical records, the population of Java has been associated with Chinese culture in the fifth century AD. It is

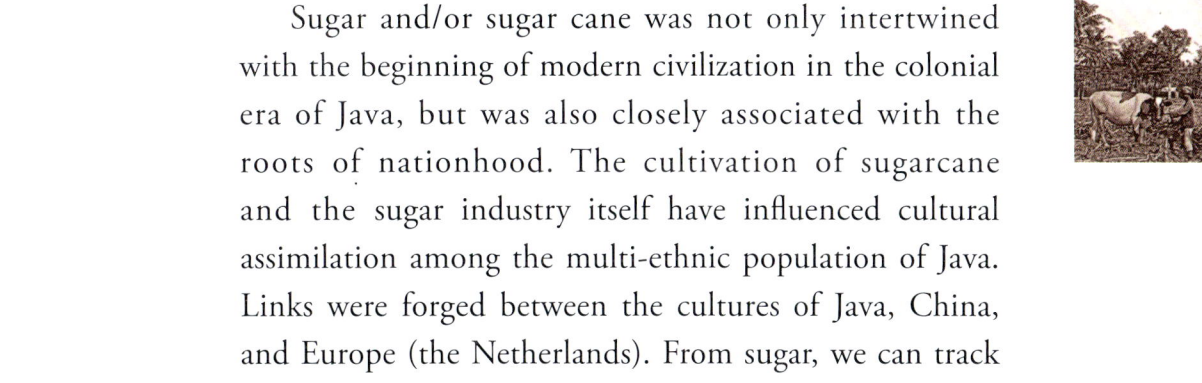

*T*he traditional atmosphere within the sugar factory. *Cembengan* is a blessing ceremony that marks the recommencement of the grinding process after a couple of months during which the factory has stopped operations while waiting for the sugarcane harvest, referred to by the Dutch as *Suiker Campagne*.

recorded that a Chinese traveller, Fa-Shien, visited Java between 412-413. Another Chinese visitor, Chau Ju-kua (1178-1225) wrote in the essay *Chu Fan Chi* (a notebook about the land of Java) that a sugar cane crop was found in Java, around Kalapa/Batavia.

The Javanese relationship with the Dutch started with the sailing expedition led by Cornelis de Houtman, which arrived at Banten in 1596. The successful voyage was made possible through de Houtman's studies of the Portuguese route in Lisbon in 1592. The arrival of de Houtman in Banten, and then in Batavia, eventually led to the formation of the Vereeningde Oost-Indische Compagnie (VOC – the Dutch East India Company) in Amsterdam in 1602. To take care of their commercial interests, the VOC, or the Company, appointed a Governor-General in Batavia, a position first held by Pieter Booth.

In January 1611, Pieter Booth made a pact with the Prince of Jayakarta. Among other provisions, the agreement entitled the VOC to use a parcel of land on the eastern side of the Ciliwung river (close to today's Pasar Ikan). The area had a population of 800 inhabitants, each receiving a wage of 1200 *Rijksdaalder* (old Dutch currency). Rijksdaalder is the equivalent of 2.5 *gulden* or *florijn*. The development of the new

Before the Dutch East India Company was established in Batavia, they first located in Banten, where the successful voyage of Cornelis de Houtman (above left) had arrived in the year 1596. That success opened a new chapter in the development of the Netherlands. De Houtman studied the economic potential of Java and determined a trade monopoly strategy through mastery of the maritime area.

Trade in Batavia became busier with the appointment of a new Governor General, Jan Pieterzoon Coen (JP Coen) (above centre) in the year 1617. He served as Governor General twice (1617-1623 and 1627-1629). Coen is regarded as the founder of Batavia. He died due to illness in 1629, the same year that Mataram invaded Batavia for the second time. Coen's body was entombed in a church, which now functions as the *Museum Wayang* in Jakarta's Old Town. Coen's headstone is still well-maintained.

Paintings showing the arrival of Dutch ships at Banten in 1596 (above right and facing page).

headquarters was intended to replace Banten, which was considered less strategic and less safe. The area formerly known as Kalapa, and then Jayakarta, was then named Batavia, derived from the Dutch *Bataaf*.

Trade in Batavia became busier with the appointment of a new Governor General, Jan Pieterzoon Coen (JP Coen) (above centre) in the year 1617. He served as Governor General twice (1617-1623 and 1627-1629). Coen is regarded as the founder of Batavia. He died due to illness in 1629, the same year that Mataram invaded Batavia for the second time. Coen's body was entombed in a church, which now functions as the *Museum Wayang* in Jakarta's Old Town. Coen's headstone is still well-maintained.

During his rule JP Coen sent an ambassador to Banten to summon the Tionghoa people. JP Coen hoped that the VOC merchant fleets in Java would become stronger through using *jung* (a type of Chinese traditional boat) owned by the Tionghoa. To enable the smooth

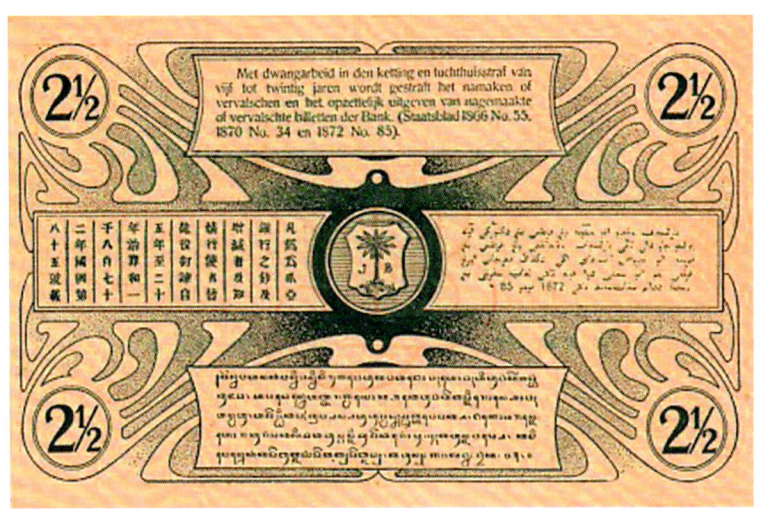

Rijksdaalder, the VOC currency was then converted into *gulden*/ *florijn*.

One *Rijksdaalder* was equivalent to 2.50 *gulden*/ *florijn* (top right).

coordination of work with the Tionghoa, from 1620 the VOC appointed one of them to be head of the residential area (*wijkmeester*) with the rank of Captain. According to historical records, the first Batavia *Kapitein der Chineezen* appointed by the VOC was So Beng Kong.

Along with the developing trade and the huge profits of the VOC, marked by the spread of silver currency (Spanish dollars) and copper coins (*Rijksdaalder*). Batavia had become a major port of Southeast Asia. This encouraged the migration of the Tionghoa people in large numbers from Tiongkok (mainland China), whether on their own initiative or brought over by the VOC to work as coolies.

Starting in 1637, the VOC exported sugar from Batavia to Europe, with more than 10,000 *pikul* per year (*pikul* is a traditional unit of measurement, now roughly equivalent to 62.5 kg). They usually bought sugar from the Tionghoa people at a price of between four to six *Rijksdaalder* per *pikul*. Besides being processed into sugar, sugar cane could also be processed into alcoholic beverages such as *arak* and rum.

The processing of turning sugar cane into sugar in the era of the VOC was still very simple, using a traditional method that can still be found in West Sumatra today, where they refer to the sugar produced as *gulo saka*. The process used a grinding machine that consisted of two cylinders made from stone or wood and placed next to each other. One of the cylinders was attached to a stick, and at the end of the stick, an animal, or sometimes a human, was tied to it to manually move the cylinder. Meanwhile, one or more persons inserted the sugar cane into the cavity between the two grinding cylinders. Nira, the substance produced by this grinding, was then poured into a large ceramic dish. The traditional sugar maker was very easy to operate and very portable,

easily transported to areas that were harvesting. In the past, sugar cane production was often found alongside rivers, as in addition to easy access to water, there was also a type of sugar cane grinder that was operated by water mills, and most importantly, in the past the rivers functioned as the arteries of trade traffic.

After its second invasion of Batavia, Mataram had an internal conflict due to long-running power struggles between the elites. Several parties in the dynasty that was established by Panembahan Senopati felt that they had a legitimate right to the throne of Mataram. The parties involved in these power struggles engaged in a protracted war. These conflicts meant that Mataram was no longer safe. For security reasons, the kingdom's capital was moved several times. The chaotic situation in Mataram had pushed the VOC to be involved in settling the conflict. The

Company used its position as an aide to the disputing royalty to ask for favourable terms, such as rights and authority over land and logistic supplies.

Summarized below are some agreements between Mataram's rulers and the Company after Sultan Agung's second defeat in his raid of Batavia, which then led to an endless feud over the throne of Mataram between 1677-1733.

Some provisions of the treaties include:

> *Exemption of customs in the territory of the VOC Mataram.*
>
> *Authority over Priangan, Pamekasan, Sumenep, and Semarang is held by the VOC.*
>
> *The expansion of VOC monopoly rights and privileges in each trade port in Mataram.*
>
> *Mataram is under the obligation to deliver 800 koyan of rice every year for a period of 25 years.*
>
> *The Company has the right to determine the selling price of wood.*
>
> *The Company has the right to determine the selling prices of cotton, food, and building materials.*
>
> *The Sunan (Sultan of Mataram) is required to fell all coffee trees, the main export of his kingdom, and his people are prohibited from growing pepper in his territory.*

The existence of these treaties established the Company as the real ruler of Mataram, which then eventually fragmented into several regions.

Furthermore, the kings in the Mataram region were in actuality merely puppets of the VOC in ruling their people. Thus, the Company became very powerful in determining who would be crowned the next King of Java. Each time a new king was to be crowned, the Company bound him to a legal contract that was disadvantageous to him and would lessen his

Facing page, top: The gold medal prize that was given by So Beng Kong to Governor-General J. Specx (1632). So Beng Kong was the first VOC-appointed *Kapitein der Chineezen* of Batavia (captain of the Chinese). *Kapitein der Chineezen* is not a military rank, but a reference to the chief of habitation (*wijkmeester*) of the Tionghoa population.

Facing page, below left: The Spanish dollar, an international currency, which was used from the time that the conquistadores set sail in the 15th century until the mid-19th century.

Above: The civil war fought between Sultan Agung and his brothers in the Kingdom of Mataram, as painted by W. Schouten (an employee of the VOC who lived in Batavia from 1658 to 1665).

The arrest of Pangeran Diponegoro,
painted by Nicolaas Pineman (1809–1860). This incident
led to the Company owning all of the land in Java.

power and authority. De facto, all of the land in Java, and all that was attached to it, belonged to the Company.

With this power over almost all of Java, it was even easier for the Company to have a monopoly over trade. All of the agricultural commodities to be exported were sold to the VOC at a very low price. Then, the Company would resell it at a very high price. Because of this, the trade in agricultural commodities became lethargic. Batavia, formerly known as a centre of sugar production, had become very quiet. A lot of farmers hesitated to grow sugarcane. Many Tionghoa people in the sugar production business went bankrupt, and many of those who lost their jobs came to Batavia. Because of this, the level of crime increased. These conditions led to the murders of Tionghoa people in large numbers in 1740, referred to as *Geger Pecinan*. These excesses had an impact as far as Kartasura, the capital of Mataram, which then led to the division of the kingdom.

Abundant profits and power with no limitation then fostered corruption in the Company. As a result, the Company also known as the VOC was declared bankrupt in 1799 and then disbanded.

*G*overnor-General Johannes van den Bosch (1830-1883), the initiator of *cultuurstelsel*, a policy directed at replenishing the state treasury after the expenditures of the Diponegoro War.

From January 1ˢᵗ 1800, the entire archipelago was merged into one region with Dutch East Indies government administration, and it was directly controlled by the Dutch government. A Governor-General, under the coordination of the Netherlands' colonial land affairs minister, led this Dutch East Indies 'State'.

During the rule of the colonial Dutch, war raged in almost all areas of the former Mataram kingdom, known as *Java-oorlog* (Java War) or Perang Diponegoro. This war between the royals occurred between 1825-1830. The war caused the death of many and cost almost all of the Dutch's government money. The war itself changed the entire face of Java. For the colonial government, war had provided them with a new oversight and massive control over the land of Java. For the native Javanese, the Diponegoro War marked the full commencement of Dutch colonialism in Java and the end of the kings in Java.

The victory of the Dutch cost them dearly, leaving them with massive quantities of debt as the state ran out of cash to finance the Diponegoro War. To pay off debts and replenish the state treasury as soon as possible, Governor-General Johannes van den Bosch created a policy of *cultuurstelsel* or Cultivation System began in 1830, shortly after the Java War ended. This system was compulsorily imposed for non-food agricultural commodities, such as coffee, rubber, quinine, indigo, and in particular sugarcane.

The principal provisions of the Cultivation System for sugarcane were:

One-fifth of rural land shall be allocated for planting sugarcane. Allocation of this land requires payment of taxes on land so that landowners are not entitled to the produce.

The Government of the Netherlands East Indies is entitled to choose the land that should be allocated for the cultivation of sugarcane.

Planting, tending and harvesting is to be conducted solely by the landowner. Landowners are rewarded based on the weight of sugar produced.

Landowners are required to transport the sugarcane to the sugar processing plant designated by the Dutch East Indies colonial government. For this they receive additional wages.

Residents who do not have the required land devote one-fifth of their working time (66 days per year) as a compulsory service without obtaining benefits.

The implementation and monitoring of the Cultivation System are conducted by government officials of the Dutch East Indies in exchange for a percentage of production (cultuur procenten).

The Cultivation System brought remarkable results. In a period of ten years, the export of sugar increased nearly ten-fold from only 6,710 tons in 1830 to 61,750 tons in 1840. In the year 1870, it

The Nederlandsche Handel Maatchappij (NHM Jakarta) office, which now serves as Museum Bank Mandiri. This was a Netherlands government-owned trading company, founded in 1824 to manage the export of Dutch East Indies plantation crops. In its development, the NHM transformed into a bank that handled plantation affairs. The NHM managed several sugar factories in Java and was also popularly known as *de Factorij* (right).

reached 146,670 tons. Sugar became the main export commodity and the main source of income for the Dutch government.

This astonishing success was supported by a state company that also functioned as a bank handling plantation issues from upstream to downstream, called *Nederlandsche Handel Maatschappij* (NHM), and founded in 1824. This company loaned capital without interest, providing engines and building infrastructure. The loan could be repaid in installments of sugar, which was then exported by the NHM. To transport the commodity, NHM also had a monopoly on ships sailing between the Dutch East Indies and Europe. Because of this monopoly, the NHM controlled organization by centralizing the bureaucracy of colonial government, from central to village level, and other facilities. Hence, the NHM was also referred to as *de Kleine* VOC (the little VOC).

The Cultivation System caused the decreased production of rice and cereal crops because some of this land was used instead for the cultivation of commercial crops such as sugarcane (and a little indigo). In the Cultivation System there were technical regulations against giving the people an education. What was needed was stricter supervision over the planting

NHM office in *Weltevereden* (Gambir), located in the Pasar Baru area of Jakarta.
This building has now been torn down (above).

workforce. The Cultivation System was a form of exploitation of the earth and people of Java. The village heads and regents, acting as stooges of the colonial government with its feudal culture, only acted to please the Dutch authorities and oppressed the people arbitrarily. The people were desperate. They had no power or thought of the word 'resistance'.

This situation evoked a strong reaction from Dutch intellectuals. One of the individuals who spoke out was Wolter Robert Baron Van Hoevel. Baron van Hoevel was a priest who was active in scientific circles as President of the Batavia Society for Arts and Scientific Knowledge. He launched a sharp critique of the Cultivation System. Consequently, the government oppressed him and eventually he chose to go home to Holland. But Baron van Hoevel's campaign on behalf of the oppressed *bumiputera* (indigenous Indonesians) did not stop there. Upon arrival in the Netherlands, Baron van Hoevel was active in political parties and criticized the government, calling on it to fix the Cultivation System that was causing misery to the people of the East Indies. Baron van Hoevel's concern was not fruitless, eventually leading to his occupying the chair of Parliament representing the Liberal Party. Through parliament Baron van Hoevel fought to replace the policy of the Cultivation System.

In addition to Baron van Hoevel's struggle, in that era (1850s) a commotion was caused in the Netherlands by a book that told the story of the long suffering people of the Dutch East Indies, caused by the Cultivation System. The book was called Max Havelaar. One part contained a fragment of *Saijah Adinda* by Multatuli. Multatuli (derived from the Latin meaning "I have suffered a lot") was the pseudonym of Eduard Douwes Dekker, who was for a few months resident assistant in Lebak,

*W*olter Baron Van Hoevel
was a pastor and President of the Batavia
Society for Arts and Scientific Knowledge.
He called on critics to reorganize
the Cultivation System, which was causing
such misery to the people.
When he represented the Liberal Party in Parliament,
he fought to replace the policy of the Cultivation System.

Banten (4 January to 23 March 1856). He was resident assistant only for some months because he uncovered the state of dilapidation of the government of Lebak's regent Raden Adipati Karta Natanegara and his inlaws. According to Multatuli, the Regent of Lebak and his inlaws had treated the people unreasonably.

As a result of this complaint, he was repatriated to the Netherlands by the government.

Please note, that in Java at the time of the Cultivation System, there was a dualism in government. The colonial government that was run by the Dutch only extended from the Governor-General to the resident assistant. From the regent and his subordinates downward, the traditional government system was used, which was run by the *bumiputera*. The Dutch "borrowed

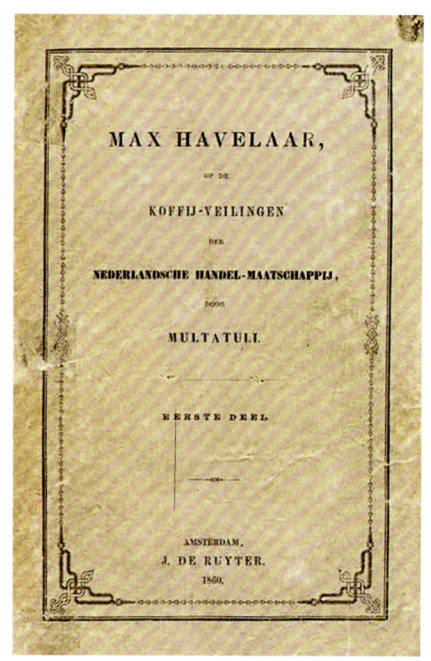

Multatuli was the pseudonym of
Eduard Douwes Dekker, which in Latin means,
'I have suffered a lot.'
He became Assistant Resident of Lebak
for only a few months before he was returned to
the Netherlands because he uncovered
the bad practices of the local government.
What Multatuli wrote was what Dekker had
experienced in Lebak, Banten (above).

Various covers of the book *Max Havelaar*,
which was translated into many languages (facing page).
It was a literary work that shook the political
universe both in the Netherlands and in Java,
delivering a strong critique of the Cultivation System,
showing the system to be immoral,
causing misery to the colonized people,
encouraging corrupt practices and stimulating
the misuse of authority. The stream of criticism
which followed was able to influence voices in Parliament,
and finally succeeded in forcing the Dutch king
to abolish the compulsory system in 1870,
after which the Agrarian Act and Sugar Act
were implemented.

the hands" of the traditional feudal government system of the *bumiputera*, which was very rigid and arbitrary. The people were not directly ruled by the Dutch government.

In his grief, Eduard Douwes Dekker wrote *Max Havelaar* in just over a month in the winter of 1859, in an inn he rented in Belgium. What Multatuli wrote is what he experienced firsthand in Lebak, Banten.

Saijah Adinda is part of the story in one chapter of *Max Havelaar*. The original title of the book is: *Max Havelaar, of de Koffie Veilingen der Nederlandsch Handelmaatschappij* or The Coffee Auctions of the Dutch Trading Company.

A short excerpt from Saijah Adinda:

Saijah's father was a peasant farmer who only had one buffalo to help plough his small field. However, this buffalo, which was his main property and was also Saijah's best friend, was confiscated by the district chief. By selling the keris, he had inherited to a Chinese man, he could buy another buffalo. But this buffalo, which was very strong and submissive, was eventually also confiscated by the district chief. When it happened, nine-year-old Saijah was in deep grief, especially because he suspected that it had been killed.

By selling his last valuable possessions, a pair of silver hooks, inherited from Saijah's mother's parents, Saijah's father could buy another buffalo. This buffalo was smaller than its predecessor, because Saijah's father did not get much money from selling the hooks. Although less strong than the confiscated buffalo, this one was very submissive to Saijah. And, as it turned out, this buffalo saved Saijah's life. He covered him with its body while defending him with his horns against the attack of a tiger on his 'little master'. Although the buffalo was injured, the tiger was killed and Saijah survived. Saijah and his father were grieved when this heroic buffalo was eventually taken away again by the district chief.

Saijah's father could no longer buy a buffalo. This meant disaster, as he would no longer be able to pay the land tax. Without the help of buffalo, ploughing the rice field would not be optimal. Yet he who can not pay land taxes should go to jail. Many peasant farmers in Saijah's village suffered a similar fate, including Adinda's father. Adinda was Saijah's neighbor, and also his future wife.

Next, as narrated by Multatuli, Saijah then left the village to look for work in Batavia, his father went to prison, while the Adinda's mother

The 2005 cover of the book *Max Havelaar*, a scene taken from the film *Saijah Adinda*, published by Djambatan, ninth reprint, translated by HB Jassin.

died and her father fled to Lampung together with a number of villagers whose buffalo was also seized by the district chief, so they could no longer pay land tax. Finally, Adinda's father and all of the villagers then joined the resistance movement in Lampung. When Saijah came home from Batavia, after successfully collecting enough money to buy three buffalo, and ready to marry Adinda, he couldn't find her. Even her house was in ruins. Finally, Saijah went to Lampung. There he found Adinda's father and three of her infant siblings dead, covered in blood. They had just been killed in a fight against the colonial soldiers. And Adinda? Her body was found naked with a chest wound, not far from her lifeless brothers.

How did Saijah react? He went to the soldiers who were still in the area and threw himself on their bayonets.

$\mathcal{C}$onrad Theodore Van Deventer (1857-1916),
was a legal expert and a member of the Dutch parliament,
and was the originator of the concept Political Ethics through
education, irrigation, and emigration. Political Ethics indicated
a political reciprocation or *de eereschuld* (debt of honor)
by the Dutch to the Dutch East Indies.
Van Deventer also established a vocational school
for women called Sekolah Kartini.

$\mathcal{A}$ foreman supervising workers digging a trench between
rows of sugarcane seedlings using the Reynoso system (above).
Reynoso is the system of sugarcane cultivation
established by Don Alvaro Reynoso from Cuba
and developed in Java since 1863.
Reynoso's sugarcane cultivation system is essentially
the technique of intensive cultivation of sugarcane
to guarantee the availability of water is more than adequate
and regulated through a good irrigation system.
In the past, the development of irrigation infrastructure was
prioritized due to the needs of the sugar industry. Staple crops
(rice) and other crops that needed irrigation must yield
to the interests of the sugar industry. Therefore, the population's
need for staple food greatly increased.

Max Havelaar was first published in 1860, a book that mirrored the societal and management processes of the colonial era. Through this book, Multatuli was trying to convey a message to the Dutch community and the colonial government, that the Cultivation System was cruel, but this crime continued as long as the dualism inherent in the patterns of colonial administration created by Van den Bosch was not removed.

Max Havelaar was scandalous at the time and aroused great social criticism, as well as rocking the political world of the Netherlands and in the land of Java. The movement against the Cultivation System was intensified because the system was considered immoral, causing misery to the people of the region and stimulate the practice of corruption and abuse of authority. The stream of criticism shaped public opinion, creating political pressure that influenced the Parliament, and finally forced the Dutch king to abolish the Cultivation

System. In addition to eliminating the Cultivation System, the Dutch government also issued a new policy, pioneered by Conrad Theodore Van Deventer (1857-1916). He initiated the concept of political ethics through education, irrigation, and emigration.

Political Ethics is a political reciprocation or *de*

eereschuld (debt of honor) by the Dutch to the East Indies. Van Deventer also established a foundation for a vocational school for women, which was given the name of *Sekolah Kartini*.

Since the abolition of the Cultivation System in 1870, economic liberalization prevailed in the Dutch East Indies, particularly with regard to the plantations. This era of economic liberalization was marked by the Agrarian Law (*Agrarische Wet*) 1870 and the Sugar Law (*Suiker Wet*) 1870. With these laws, the private sector had a huge opportunity and certainty of law, which then resulted in an inevitable liberalization of the sugar plantations. However, the Cultivation System of sugarcane actually ended slowly by the year 1890.

The Sugar Law of 1870 mainly mentioned that private entrepreneurs had been given the right to lease land for 75 years (*hak erfpacht*). People were allowed to lease out their land for a maximum of 35 years for wetland and 12.5 years for dry land. In short, the Sugar Law ended the monopoly of the sugarcane plantations and the sugar factories owned by the government. Along with the implementation of the Agrarian Law, the land ownership rights of the *bumiputera* were recognized by the government.

The policy of economic liberalization led to the emergence of private entrepreneurs, such as the legendary figure Oei Tiong Ham, the son of a Semarang businessman named Oei Tjie-Sin, whose nickname was Kian Gwan. Oei Tiong Ham was born in 1866 and died in Singapore in 1924. He was also known as the king of sugar. Oei Tiong Ham Concern (OTHC), owned by Oei Tiong Ham, was the first transnational conglomerate from Southeast Asia. In 1910, OTHC had already opened branches in London, Amsterdam and other Asian countries. Within five years, OTHC sold 725,000 tons of sugar to Europe, Asia, and America.

*O*ey Tiong Ham (1866-1924),
a Semarang tycoon known as the king of sugar.

His fame as an entrepreneur who could penetrate market boundaries of that size has been unmatched until now. He had five sugar factories in Central Java and East Java. The company was taken over by the Government of Indonesia through a decision of the Semarang Economic Court on July 10, 1961. The native sugar tycoon was Kanjeng Gusti Adipati Aryo (KGPAA) Mangkunegara IV (1811-1881). He built two factories in Surakarta, namely Colomadu (1857) and Tasikmadu (1867).

Other than these two leading figures of Java, there was a large Dutch company also in operation. HVA (Handelsvereeniging Amsterdam) was an Amsterdam merchant union that played a major role in various plantations.

Along with the progress of the sugar industry and commerce, infrastructure was also growing. Road networks and railroads grew fast, connecting the rapidly growing economic centers and sugar producing regions. The modern sugar industry grew like mushrooms in the rainy season. As of 1890 there were 151 sugar factories in Java, with a total area of 44,933 hectares.

Due to economic liberalization, the sugar industry

*K*GPAA Mangkunegara IV (1811-1881),
the first bumiputera (indigenous Indonesian) to own a sugar factory.

was entirely controlled by the private sector. The liberal economic system had also led to a sharp increase in production of sugar for export, from only 146.6 thousand tons in 1870 to 736.6 thousand tons in 1900. By the time of the big economic depression in 1930, sugar production in Java had increased to 2.3 million tons. At that time, the Dutch East Indies (Indonesia) was the second biggest sugar exporter in the world after Cuba. Even so, the fast development of the sugarcane industry was not free from obstacles and challenges. Tight competition came from the sugar beet industry, which already controlled the European

*T*he sugarcane seedlings selection process. Photo from 1920 (top right).

*T*he traditional sugar-making process using a simple tool driven by animal power (oxen) in Tulung Agung, East Java. Photo from 1920 (center).

*T*ransportation of sugarcane in the vicinity of the river Brantas in East Java (bottom).

sugar market and was capable of producing better quality sugar. Especially when the epidemic of *sereh* disease almost destroyed the sugar industry in Java. Sugar entrepreneurs realized the need for a research institution that could find a way to counter the obstacles to production and also find a solution to the challenges of marketing in Europe. They established a research institute called POJ (*Proefstation Oost Java*). POJ then became one of the pioneers in the establishment of the International Society of Sugarcane Technologists (ISSCT), an association of world-renowned sugar experts focused on sugarcane cultivation and technological research in the sugar industry. POJ is now called the Indonesian Sugar Research Institute (*Pusat Penelitian Perkebunan Gula Indonesia*, P3GI).

In 50 years' time (1887-1941), POJ, located in Pasuruan, had become the world's most prominent sugar research center. Research into sugarcane cultivation and the techniques of sugar processing thrived. The results of the POJ research could be directly applied and fully utilized by all sugar factories in Java. One of POJ's international achievements was discovering POJ 2878, a top variety of sugarcane also known as 'wonder cane' or 'magic sugarcane'. The quality of the POJ 2878 sugarcane can be observed from the large tall stems, reaching up to four feet, with a level of productivity that other varieties have not matched until now.

That's the story of the sugarcane from the 'paradise land' of Java, the result of the trade of which was used to build the Netherlands. No wonder the renowned Dutch historian Cornelis Fasseur referred to sugarcane as "the cork on which the Netherlands floats".

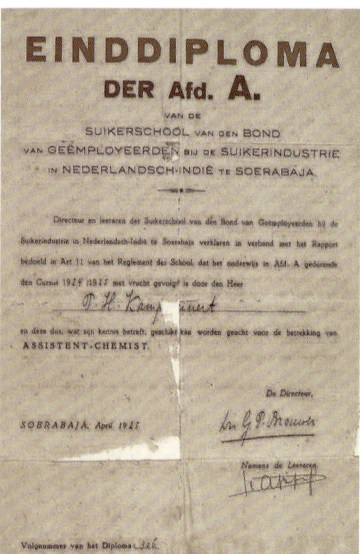

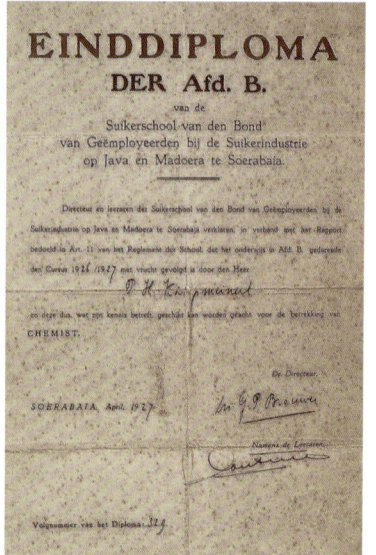

*T*he diploma for chemists in former times was called
the "sugar doctor" diploma.
The graduates worked in the laboratory to test product quality.
The *afdeling A* diploma was for assistant chemists.
The *afdeling B* diploma was for chemists (*chemiker*).
The schools for chemists were organized by *Algemeene Syndicaat
van Suikerfabriekanten in Nederlandsche Indie* (ASSI),
a sugar syndicate based in Surabaya.

*T*he working atmosphere in the sugar factory.

Among other photos: The administrative office at PG Ketanen Mojokerto (1906).

PG is an abbreviation of the Indonesian *Pabrik Gula*, or Sugar Factory.

*T*he working atmosphere in the sugar factory. Among others:

Photos of employees at PG Tasikmadoe Karanganyar Mangkunegaran (1930).

The office at PG Goedo, Jombang (1935).

The office at PG Mritjan, Kediri (1930).

The *Ambacht* school (a carpentry technical school) opened to fill the needs of skilled craftsmen;

some sugar factories opened this school close to the factory location.

Pictured above are students from the *Ambacht* school at PG Peterongan Jombang at work (1925).

*T*he process of plant breeding through crossing seeds in *Het Proefstation Oost Java*, Pasuruan in 1937;
this process is conducted to create the best possible seeds.
One of the results of this research was the POJ 2878 sugarcane variety or the so-called *wondercane*,
which grew as high as 4 meters and with a diameter much larger than other sugarcane varieties at the time.

A cultural expression.

One part of this traditional ceremony is to parade a sugarcane bride and groom during the grinding party

at PG Gayam/Pasuruan (*below*), accompanied by a social dance, a *tayuban* at PG Modjopanggoeng (*above*).

The ceremony has become customary in the sugarcane society until now.

Photo circa 1920.

$\mathscr{P}$G Tangerang Oost, one of the sugar factories in the region of Bondowoso that was relocated from around Batavia
and Pamanoekan to *Oosthoek*.
Locomotives and inspections train at PG Dajtiroto (1935).
Photos of employees of PG Tasikmadoe, owned by the Mangkunegaran principality (circa 1930).

*S*ome photos of now defunct buildings with magnificent
architecture, among others:

The official housing at PG Peterongan, 1930

The Polyclinic at PG Nganjuk, 1930

The official housing at PG Poppoh Sidoardjo, 1920

Club house at PG Bagoe, Probolinggo, 1915

PG Soember Kareng Kraksaan, Probolinggo, 1900.

*B*eautiful buildings that are now a distant memory:

The office at PG Ketanen Modjokerto, 1925 (top).

The house of the head administrator at PG Peterongan Djombang, 1925.

Official housing at PG Perning Mojokerto, East Java, 1920.

Photos of Surabaya dating from the 1930s.

Kembang Jepun (Chinatown), Surabaya

De Roode Brug (Red Bridge)

Pecinan Kulon (around *Kembang Jepun*)

Jalan Gula (Sugar Road)

THE MARCH OF SUGAR

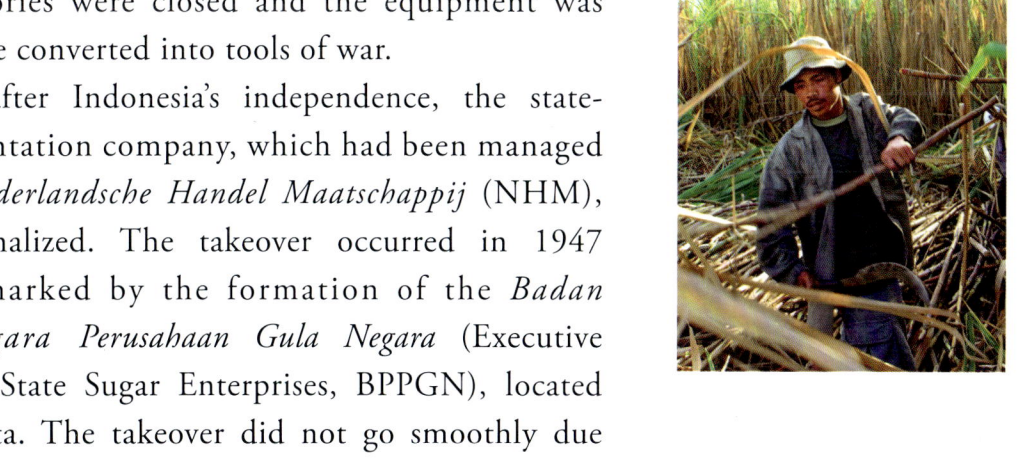

During World War II, the Pacific War resulted in the Dutch losing their power over the Dutch East Indies. The colonial government of the Dutch East Indies was soon replaced by the occupation of the Japanese army. During the occupation of the Japanese army, sugar production fell sharply in Java. Most of the sugar factories were closed and the equipment was seized to be converted into tools of war.

Soon after Indonesia's independence, the state-owned plantation company, which had been managed by the *Nederlandsche Handel Maatschappij* (NHM), was nationalized. The takeover occurred in 1947 and was marked by the formation of the *Badan Penyelenggara Perusahaan Gula Negara* (Executive Board for State Sugar Enterprises, BPPGN), located in Surakarta. The takeover did not go smoothly due to resistance from the Netherlands through the Dutch military police in 1947 and 1949.

The result of the Round Table Conference (RTC) in Den Haag in 1949, had given private Dutch plantation companies the opportunity to resume operations. But it did not last long because all assets of foreign companies (mainly Dutch) were nationalized in 1957. Plantations formerly owned by the Dutch were regulated by Government Regulation No. 24 1958. Furthermore, these companies were then grouped into *Perusahaan Perkebunan Negara* (State-Owned Agricultural Enterprises, PPN), which later became *Perseroan Terbatas Perkebunan Negara* (Limited Liability State-Owned Agricultural Enterprises, PTPN), and has

*R*ows of lorries laden with sugarcane ready for grinding in the *emplasemen* (field where the lorry is parked) at PG Wonolangan, Probolinggo.

A carpet of young sugarcane, from the PG Djatiroto Lumajang HGU (Business Use Right). PG Djatiroto, built in 1910, was the largest sugar factory in Java that still had land adequate for HGU.

now been reintegrated into 14 *Perseroan Terbatas Perkebunan Nusantara* (State-Owned Plantation Enterprises, PTPN). The state-owned plantation companies generally grew several types of commodity (multi-crops); only PTPN XI (Persero) focused on the single commodity of sugar. The Company, with headquarters in Surabaya, currently manages 17 sugar factories, one of which is not in operation.

Although there are several new sugar factories, since 1967 Indonesia has become a net importer of sugar. Currently, Indonesia is the second largest importer of sugar, second after the Russian Federation. On the other hand, some countries that originally studied the Java sugar industry, such as Thailand and Australia, have now become the world's leading sugar producers.

The problems of increasing population, the lack of land and the increase in education, played a role in influencing the sugarcane farmers' decisions on what to grow on their land. After experiencing a variety of policies, such as the rental system, sharing system, and the *Tebu Rakyat Intensifikasi* (smallholders' sugarcane intensification program, TRI), which was mandatory and binding, nowadays the farmer has more freedom in determining the types of crops they wish to grow. Now, farmers are faced with more rational options. Whether the farmer will plant cereals, rice, or sugarcane, depends on cost-benefit considerations and the relative risks of these choices.

This is of course a challenge for the managers of the sugar industry in their attempts to reach production targets. It means that all of the sugar plantation companies (especially PTPN) have to intervene in order to persuade farmers to plant sugarcane. Of course the problem is not that simple. The government has continuously made regulations to increase the production of sugar as well as to improve the welfare of farmers, but until now the condition of the sugar industry remains sluggish.

Indeed, the situation is very different when compared with what has happened in the past. Times have changed, problems that arise are different and more complex.

As someone who enjoys history, I know that the sugarcane plantation was the belle of the colonial era economy. It left many traces of history, such as landscape and architecture, the atmosphere of the beautiful estates, and of course other important factors that we can learn from.

I would like to invite the reader to gain a new perspective on the sugar plantations as a part of our culture. I believe many Indonesian people do not know their own country very well. Many have never set foot in the plantation areas. Therefore this 'march of sugar' would be helpful in getting to know more about the situation of the plantations that extend through the vast lush greenery of the countryside. The experience of riding on a lorry in the middle of the sugarcane plantation, and other things that we rarely see in the city, all these are part of the nation's cultural assets.

The beautiful, spacious, and shady houses and the beautiful scenery are part of the current 'march of sugar'.
The well-maintained house of the administrator, includes the old machines built in the 1800s and the sugar warehouse which was an inheritance from a British plantation company that is now PG Wonolangan, Probolinggo, currently still operating.
Some of these objects are invaluable assets. Let's get to know the fertile land of the country, the gorgeous plantation land that holds a million memories and hope!

*R*aking, raising soil and clearing weeds using 'cow power' is a technique of crop cultivation that has been around for hundreds of years, and is still used at PG Djatiroto. In order to prevent the cows from eating the plants, the mouth is muzzled. A very unique sight.

The sweet flavors we enjoy partly come from here and from the hard work of peasant farmers who lead a simple life, using simple working tools, *caping* and *arit* (a broad woven bamboo hat and a sickle).

The process of harvesting sugarcane in Java is mostly still done manually, because many factories rented relatively small plots of land to the peasant farmers. However, some have been mechanized, such as privately owned sugar factories outside Java.

*M*any varieties of sugarcane are cultivated to produce sugar. One of the many varieties that are cultivated today is the BL (Bululawang) type, developed in the Bululawang plantation in Malang. This type of sugarcane has high resistance to pests and diseases with relatively low maintenance costs.

*S*ugarcane land that has been harvested is left to grow before being harvested the following season. This system is called *ratoon* or *keprasan*.

Gotong-royong (mutual assistance)

To facilitate the transportation of sugarcane from the plantation, a temporary railway is needed along
which the lorry can run. Cows or buffaloes are used to transport a sugarcane-laden lorry from the plantation
to the permanent railway line, a distance of between 100-300m.

*C*hallenges.

The special trains and lorries used to carry sugarcane have now been replaced by other modes
of transport such as trucks. This was caused by the reduced coverage of the railway network.
The decreased usage of the special train was due to reasons such as the reduction of the garden area
surrounding the factory, the absence of an adequate maintenance budget, and theft.
Daunting challenges to the efforts to boost the production of sugar.

'*Tak kenal maka tak sayang*'

(this could be translated as 'the less known, the less loved').

It's as if this photo captures the millions of stories about sugar for our children

and grandchildren, so that we can continue to be a strong, self-sufficient nation.

The lorry and the scale are the determining parts in the sugar manufacturing process.

This is not just any scale; this one is used to determine the price of sugarcane to be bought from the farmers. After being weighed, the sugarcane is ground. The *nira* (sap) that results from the grinding process is analyzed. The outcome of this analysis then determines the amount of money that must be paid to the farmers that own the sugarcane. The analysis is called the individual yield analysis.

The conventional process of cooling down heated water from the machine at PG Wonolangan (*facing page and above*),
and the modern water-cooling process at PG Semboro, Jember (*below*).
The cooled water is then reused, creating a continuous circulation.

Nothing is wasted in the sugar production process. The initial process of grinding the sugarcane entails putting weighed stacks of sugarcane into the grinding machine. This refining process will result in raw *nira* (sap) and *bagasse* (fibrous residue), which can then be processed into fuel or paper.

*C*lockwise:

Three factories that played a part in the history of the sugar industry in Java

1. PG Djatiroto was built in 1910. It was the largest sugar factory in Java, formerly owned by HVA.

2. PG Redjo AgungBaru, the first sugar factory run on electricity, belonged to OTHC (Oei Tiong Ham Concern).

3. PG Colomadu, the first sugar factory owned by a *bumiputera* or indigenous Indonesian (Mangkunegara IV), was established in 1857 and stopped operating in 1998.

The sugar manufacturing process, starting from grinding, to purification, evaporation,
cooking, screening, and packaging.
The grinding process produces raw *nira* (sap) and pulp.
Purification is a process of cleaning the sap of dirt.
The purification of raw *nira* is carried out by adding a variety
of substances to precipitate the dirt, resulting in the purified *nira*.

*V*aporization: evaporating the purified *nira* into sugar syrup.

Cooking: boiling the sugar syrup to produce raw sugar.

Screening: the sugar is screened to separate the raw sugar crystals and the molasses.

Packaging: sugar crystals are packed in sacks or plastic bags according to the size that will be sold to the market.

By-products such as molasses are sold in bulk form, as are other industrial raw materials (*monosodiumglutamate/* MSG, alcohol and spirits, liquor, mixed fodder, and so forth).

"*H*olobis kuntul baris"
A call often uttered by the porters at work, to keep their concerted movements in rhythm.

Wonolangan is an old factory with a machine made in the 1800s that is still fully functioning, with some natural support. Could it be possible for us not to import sugar?

The residences of sugar factory employees in East Java.

Rumah Panggung, the high-floored houses found at PG Djatiroto, are designed to protect inhabitants from any dangers posed by wild creatures such as snakes and also from flooding. The location of PG Djatiroto used to be a marshy area.
(*Facing page, above right*).

The East Indies architecture is characteristic of the sugar factory residences at PG De Maas in Situbondo, with large pillars and sky-high ceilings to suit the tropical climate.
(*Facing page, bottom left*).

Details of the facade of the head administrator's house at the Wonolangan Probolinggo sugar factory. With a high roof supported by carved pillars, a typical feature of the East Indies empire colonial style architecture, and also of the British planters. Located on the highway from Surabaya to Banyuwangi (*de Groote Postweg*), this building still retains the friendly welcoming ambience of the past.

$\mathcal{S}$ome of the vintage furniture that still decorates many of the big houses.

A variety of patterned tiles adorn them.

If you have the chance to stay here, it is as if you're rewinding back the past, especially when you hear the strong wind of Probolinggo, which comes in the nights from June to September. The roar of the wind, called *angin gending*, breaks the silence of the night.

The family cemetery of Charles Etty Esq. is still visited regularly by his heirs from Europe (UK).
Etty was a captain of British sugar who succeeded in developing the sugar industry in Kolkata (Calcutta), India
and expanded to Java by establishing the Wonolangan sugar factory.
The modernization of the sugar industry occurred when the British occupied Java (1811-1815). Lieutenant-Governor Raffles invited
English entrepreneurs who had done well in Kolkata to invest in Java. Originally attempted in West Java
(around Pamanukan Subang), it failed there and the sugar industry was eventually successfully developed in *Oosthoek*.

The administrator's house at PG De Maas is still graceful and grand, standing firm amidst the old trees. If we approach the balcony of this building, with the view of the broad expanse of fields and mountains, its calming effects are undeniable. If this building, which has not been inhabited since the factory closed, were to be used appropriately, perhaps blessings would also flow through here.

$\mathcal{S}$ugar factories were in the past the driving forces of modernization for the surrounding area. The presence of the sugar factory usually brought with it modern infrastructure such as a road network, railways, bridges, education facilities, and hospital facilities. One of the few remaining and maintained facilities left is the HVA Toeloengredjo Hospital, Pare Kediri. The legacy of the HVA hospital dates back to 1908, and it is now managed by PTPN X (Persero). It became one of the leading hospitals in the district of Kediri. Notice the pillar details, the colors and shapes that are blended with the natural form of the window to create a tasteful style of architecture.

It is no surprise that such a large hospital is located in Kediri, as in the past
this area had many sugar factories, one of the largest of which was Pesantren.
It is an impressive building, still intact and functioning well, while telling a story of the past
of the town of Kediri and surrounding areas.

Maintaining old buildings is certainly not easy and it is very costly. Due appreciation should be given to the management of this *Indies*-style hospital, which maintained the aesthetics of the building and the environment. Bamboo shades, open terraces and a sloping roof supported by pillars, add charm to this tropical building. In addition, the large and tall windows, which are now rarely found in a city with increasing crowds and pollution.

*T*he unique sight of the employee residences
at the Tasikmadoe factory. The factory, originally
owned by Mangkunegara IV, is now a successful
agro-tourism site. When the holiday season comes,
visitors are abundant. Perhaps there is a reading room
about the history of sugar in Tasikmadoe?
Hopefully so.

At a glance, this building might not look like as though it's located in the village of Karanganyar, Surakarta.
When compared with the surrounding environment, the Mangkunegara IV-owned factory building (*above*) is very modern
and striking. Surakarta was formerly known as *Vorstenlanden*, which means an area under the kingdom.
The land and also the residents in the territory of the kingdom were not bound by the Cultivation System policy.
Currently, the Tasikmadoe sugar factory is known by local people by the name Sondokoro,
a village in Karanganyar where the factory was located.

Today, even with limited resources, the dedication of P3GI (*right*) still leads to the production of superior varieties of
sugarcane, such as sugarcane varieties for drought-resistant land. It is not impossible that in the future beneficial research
results will emerge from the work of P3GI, such as the use of sugarcane for energy, as is found in developed countries.

SUGAR TOWN

Pasuruan, in *Oosthoek*, was once dubbed 'sugar town'. *Oosthoek* is a Dutch word referring to the area on the eastern tip of Java where the island of Java narrows, from Pasuruan to the Bali Strait. In the era of the VOC, this region was a plantation paradise. *Oosthoek* is often called *emas hijau*, or 'green gold', as many other industrial crops, such as coffee, tobacco, cotton, teak forests and others can be found there. *Oosthoek /eastern salient/bang wetan/east end*, is the region that includes Pasuruan, Probolinggo (Banger), Situbondo (Panarukan), Besuki (including Bondowoso, Jember), Lumajang and Banyuwangi (Blambangan).

Pasuruan, which was in the VOC archives spelt Pasuruwan or Pesuruwan, while the British wrote *Passarouang* (money market), is a small town on the eastern tip of Java that was very crowded with trade traffic. It consists of the local autonomous government, Pasaruan Municipality and Pasuruan Regency. In addition to the heritage railway network of the Dutch era, the city has also had a port since the days of the empire of Airlangga of Kediri. It is therefore no surprise that Pasuruan also has a multi-ethnic population. Besides Chinese and Europeans, many people of Arab descent also came from Pasuruan (from the Bangil area). According to historical records, some of those who spread Islam in Java (*Wali Songo*) were descended from Hadrami (the people of Hadramaut, such as Sunan Ampel and Sunan Giri). They generally lived in coastal areas and worked as traders.

In Pasuruan the remains of elegant houses that resemble palaces are still to be found next to each other

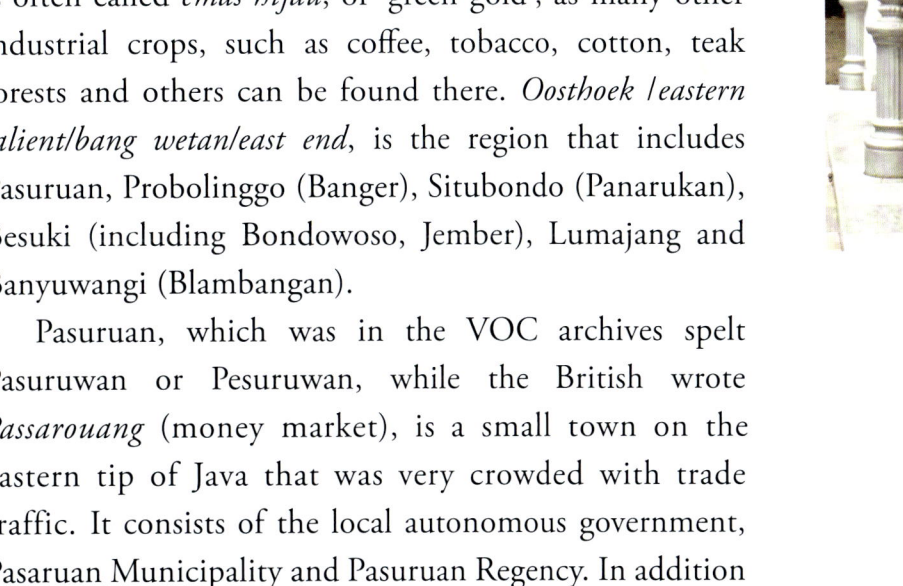

A palace-like house from the mid-nineteenth century, owned by the *Kapitein der Chineezen* Tan Kong Seng, which is still maintained by his heirs. A treasury of culture that still vibrates with history.

along the highway from Surabaya to Banyuwangi, on the route to Bali. Most of the buildings have today changed their function. In fact, many have also changed shape, but the rest of the beautiful buildings there are also still well-maintained, as can be witnessed in this book.

Oosthoek, Probolinggo and the Han family

Because Pasuruan was located in *Oosthoek*, the development of this region can not be viewed separately from the district of Probolinggo, which was previously named Banger in the VOC era, the capital of *Oosthoek*. Probolinggo was a city owned by two brothers, Han Chan Piet and Han Kik Ko, sons of Surabaya's *Kapitein der Chineezen* Han Bwe Kong (1727-1778). The land was purchased from Governor-General Daendels and Lieutenant-Governor Thomas Stamford Raffles.

The father of the *Kapitein der Chineezen*, Han Siong Kong (1673 - 1743), lived in Lasem, an area on the north coast of Central Java which was adjacent to the East Java Province. He died in Rajegwesi, now Bojonegoro. Han Siong Kong, whose ancestors came from Fu Jian, China, had five children (all born in Lasem). One of them, Han Tjien Kong (1720-1776), had a Javanese name, Surio Prenolo, and converted to Islam. He married many Javanese and Peranakan girls. His family developed and inherited the 'tradition of leadership', becoming hereditary heads of the region (*Majoor, Kapitein, Liutenant de Chineezen*) in Surabaya

*H*an's family tree, which includes a lot of landlords in East Java, is kept in the same house where the ashes of the Han family are stored, on Jalan Karet, Surabaya (*above left*).

*P*robolinggo banknotes (Probolinggo *papier*), a new type of banknote issued at the suggestion of Daendels to overcome the scarcity of coins at the time of the land transactions between the Netherlands Government and the brothers Han Chan Piet and Han Kik Ko.

and some areas in East Java, Central Java and even as far as Kutaraja Aceh.

The brothers Han Chan Piet and Han Kik Ko, sons of the *Kapitein der Chineezen*, bought thousands of hectares of land between 1810 and 1813, which covered several residencies, Besuki-Panarukan and Probolinggo, with the privileges inherent in that region. Among others were teak forest property rights over land, rights to collect residential taxes and the tax commission from the Dutch Government, as well as easy access. The agreed price was 100,000 Spanish dollars, payable in installments over 10 years without interest. He was appointed in an official ceremony as the Chinese Mayor (*Majoor der Chineezen*) and the Landlord of Probolinggo, as well as a Javanese traditional ruler or regent at the time, titled *Tumenggung* (a middle rank of the Javanese nobility), which later became known as *Tumenggung*

A painting of Probolinggo by JWB Wardenaar, a Semarang-born Dutch citizen (1785-1864).

Babah (indicating a Chinese *Tumenggung*). From this *Tumenggung Babah* in Probolinggo, came generations of descendents that at that time controlled the sugar industry and many other trades.

Besides being businessmen, many of the descendents of Han became regents under the name of a Javanese aristocrat, like Raden Adipati Soeroadinegoro (Babah Sam/Han Sam Kong), who was the regent of Malang and Tuban (1808-1818), and Raden Soero Adiwikromo, regent of Besuki and Jember (1776 and 1796), who married a noblewoman from Sumenep Madura.

Aside from being a trading town, the town of Pasuruan is also a very famous city of the VOC era, because it was the hiding place of Surapati, a sworn enemy of the Company. Surapati was a slave before joining the army of the Company and had learned many war strategies from it. Because of a forbidden love affair with a VOC general's daughter, he was expelled. After his expulsion, he joined the Javanese royal army (Kartasura), developing strength and succeeding in killing Captain Tack, after which he ran to Pasuruan. There he built the Surapati kingdom (1686-1706). In the end he was killed by soldiers of the Company, his body was burned and the ashes thrown into the sea.

Pasuruan is better known for its development as a busy trading town. Located on the coast, it has a long history since the days of Airlangga, and is also an area close to the 'center' of the Tionghoa community (Lasem), with a long history with the Tionghoa landlords, and therefore the town of Pasuruan city has a distinctive character. When viewed from the history of acculturation or cultural assimilation of the Chinese in Java, which is so strong, it is not surprising that most of the Chinese adapted to the Javanese way of living. One example is that they called their master *ndoro nyo* (*ndoro sinyo*, for men) and *ndoro non* (*ndoro nonik*, for women). They also adopted the routines of everyday life that were appropriate to *priyayi* in Java. In addition, they collected works of art such as *keris*, *wayang*, *gamelan* and so forth. Such homes can witnessed in this book, such as the family house of the *Kapitein der Chineezen* Tan Kong Seng. This house is located on Jalan Hasanudin, known by locals as the house of *Insinyur Kwee*, grandson of the Pasuruan *Kapitein der Chineezen*. He graduated from Bandung's *Technische Hoogeschool*, now known as ITB (Bandung Institute of Technology). After that he continued his studies in the Netherlands, and all his life dedicated himself to a company specializing in construction and fabrication, "de Bromo" Pasuruan, which later became the state-owned company PT Boma Bisma Indra. Now he is already deceased.

The style of this house is a mixture of different elements, Chinese, Javanese, European, commonly referred to as eclecticism, a way of designing that picks and chooses various kinds of details of the styles of the past that are fascinating and interesting, and then combined into a significant element for the new building.

They designed this house differently to those found in Chinatown in other regions. Viewed from the outside, it looks like a house in Europe, but once inside, a shrine can be seen, filled with small sculptures and a family tree, located right in the middle between the living room and family room.

According to Handinoto (lecturer at the Petra Christian University, Surabaya), this mix of Chinese and European architecture that can be found in Pasuruan is not common in other coastal cities of Java, and therefore this architectural style of Pasuruan's Chinatown could be referred to as *'The Chinese of Pasuruan Style'*.

For the sugar society of the world, Pasuruan was known as 'the holy city of sugar', because it had complete research institutions, from pre-production to post-production of sugar (*Proefstation Oost Java*) which is now named P3GI, an abbreviation of *Pusat Penelitian Perkebunan Gula Indonesia* (Indonesian Sugar Research Institute). This research institution was in the past a model for the sugar industry in the rest of the world.

Hopefully the photographs of this Sugar Town 'legacy' will inspire us to appreciate old buildings as a part of Indonesia's wealth of culture and become a source of learning for the current generation and a tourist attraction. And, more importantly, as a medium to stimulate interest in the history of the town and to develop a sense of belonging.

*V*arious details of architectural elements, decorative elements, and interior and exterior views of houses in Pasuruan.
An example of the cultural expression of the nation.

This beautiful house, built in 1800, was originally owned by a citizen of the Netherlands and sold to a Tionghoa businessman in the year 1840. The house is located on the main road of Pasuruan. Owned by Tan Kong Seng, *Kapitein der Chineezen*, it has been renovated by a Dutch architect to its current condition. Today the local Pasuruan people know it as the house of *Insinyur* (Engineer) Kwee.

*V*arious garden ornaments such as statues and European-style lamps are located in the spacious backyard,
a very beautiful scene.
The form of the *Joglo* terrace roof is typically characteristic of houses from the old Javanese aristocracy,
with a combination of architecture similar to European houses from the front,
while from the back of the house has the appearance of a home of a "Javanese Duke".

Who would think that this very European-style house is located in Pasuruan? The Italian marble floors and sturdy iron fence were imported directly from the country of origin, after the 20 years that the house was owned by *Kapitein* Tan Kong Seng in the year 1860. It is indeed a charming piece of Pasuruan history that should be protected as a building of cultural heritage.

The upper window decoration (*bovenlicht*) with European-style paintings on doors combined with Chinese motifs, side by side with a door complete with vent and cabinet with classical Javanese kris, reflecting the homeowner's perspective of diversity. A reflection of the openness of character of a tolerant nation.

*A*n altar for prayers acts as the separator between the intermediary space (*midden galeri*) and family rooms, with furniture supplied from China and lights from Italy; this is part of the heritage of this house along with a set of gamelan, which is still treated in accordance with the customs of the Javanese as a heirloom. This is a "Chinese Pasuruan" house, with a mixture of elements from China, Java, and Europe, in a style commonly called eclecticism, a form of design through integration by taking a variety of details from various styles of the past that are fascinating and interesting, then combining them in architectural harmony.

*E*very day this house, which nowadays is one of the icons of Pasuruan architecture, is decorated with flowers that grow in the garden, adding beauty to this *'Njawani'* (Javanese-style) corner of the room. A blend of elegant interiors.

125

*M*agnificently special.
The blue Venetian glass and its shutters, as well as
the decorated ceramic floors, walls, up to the ceiling.
Everything came from Italy. When the house was
purchased from the Dutch in 1840, its condition
was not as good as this; there is only a piano left.
Notice the Italian shutters (blue Venetian glass)
combined directly with the silver-painted wood,
a very modern touch at that time.

*N*ot only special from the outside,
this is the private room of the *Kapitein der Chineezen*,
who also was king of real estate.
The combination of the marble sink
and brass iron bed complements
the exquisite features in this room,
which overlooks the garden.

*V*arious motifs of the Italian marble floor, which looks like a colorful carpet,

decorating each room with different shades.

A rare glimpse of an antique house that is well maintained along with all its contents!

Extraordinary!!

*A*part from a very beautiful terrace
that was added to this building,
there are also *gandhok* houses
to the left and right,
which connect to the main building,
a feature typical of the classical Javanese
houses owned by aristocrats,
referred to as "*ayu, ayom, ayem*"
or "*beautiful, shaded, tranquil*".
Notice the 'lace' on the terrace and
the roof of the *gandhok* roof
that serves as a shield from wind, rain and light.
Romantic, isn't it?

The *Kapitein der Chineezen* also held the rights over all pawnshop licenses in Pasuruan,
as well as other privileges, so it is understandable if the house he built resembles a small palace in Europe, especially
given the fact that Pasuruan's status as a commercial port city made it easier to bring in the imported goods.
It's possible that, due to the hectic trading in Pasuruan, it was in former times called *'pasar uang'* ('money market').

*I*nspirations that continue to entice.

Various details from styles of the past, harmoniously positioned, in a house that has witnessed much history.

A very long chain of reminders of the "traces of sugar" over time.

The lion, a symbol of the Dutch government (*Dutch Leeuw Van Oranje*), was made into a very expressive sculpture in front of the house of the *Kapitein der Chineezen* of Pasuruan. In the 19th century, *Le Style Empire* became a style commonly used in the Dutch East Indies. It was a style influenced by the French that reached Indonesia when Daendels became Governor-General of the Dutch East Indies.

The year in which this house of a sugar entrepreneur was built is unknown, since it has changed owners since 1938. In the 1930s, the years of global economic depression affected the sugar price and resulted in a significant drop in sugar prices and subsequent losses to the sugar entrepreneurs, causing the sugar company to go out of business. All company assets, including this house, were sold by the entrepreneurs to the family of Arab descent Bin Thalib.

The homeowner added Arabic lettering that reads 'Darussalam', which means the house is open to everyone. Occupying an area of 3500 m², the house was originally owned by a Tionghoa citizen and had a diverse architectural style, with a Chinese-style roof at the rear, an ornate *entablatur* with a European-style *akroterion* on the front edge of the roof, strengthened with the long hallway with rows of arcade pillars, which features a short fence at the bottom (*balustrade*).

"The "curtain of trees" as a shield from dust and light is really appealing to anyone who passes! It's not only a beautiful house but it's also very shady, which we can feel when we enter the garden. The high pavilions situated on either side of the yard has not been renovated but is still neat and clean, while retaining a function as a shield from the heat and the glare of the sun.

$\mathcal{P}$art of the greatest appeal of old buildings is in the details!

Note the detailed ornamentation on the park lamps, the roof, the sunscreen of carved wood on the front porch,

matching the color of the doors, and the details of the neat and sturdy water pipes.

The landlord was very careful in choosing furniture that matched.
All of the elements, from doors to other antique furniture, have an Art Deco style and are harmoniously
arranged on this East Indies-style porch, creating the impression that the space is very modern.

A large table of dimensions 5.5 m. x 1.5 m., and a charming woven antique chair
inherited from the old owner, is one of the beauties of this spacious and bright house.
Breezy winds in the town of Pasuruan cradle us inside,
imagining the atmosphere of the past.

Various interior details of the Darussalam house can be seen on the divider that separates the praying altar and the living room. *Chi lin* is an animal believed to be a vehicle of the gods, with the body of horse and a head of dragon, and it symbolizes loyalty, strength, ambition, and control of competition. The carp symbolizes success, because it struggles against the flow of the river.

$\mathcal{T}$he light that slips through the stained glass during the day, blended with the European-style painting of the roof, as found on page 149, adds to the romantic atmosphere of this beautiful bedroom.

$\mathcal{A}$ swiftlet house (in which species of the bird are raised and their nests used for bird's nest soup) is located to the right and left of this house, in the front yard. Formerly, this house functioned as a family pavilion, but it is now used as a swiftlet house (*below*). The corridors on the left and right of the house were a very common detail of buildings at the time because this was one way to create shelter from the sun.

This house, built in 1925, has very beautiful architectural detail. It is located on the road to Banyuwangi from Pasuruan, Java, which is called the Soekarno-Hatta road. Because of its uniqueness, this house is often used as a reference for architecture students. The detailed design of the lightning rod, the fence lamps, and the park, adds an impressive charm to the exterior.

As architecture developed between 1910-1920,
it was the era of architectural eclecticism,
which was a blend of architecture that takes on
various styles, as in this house that incorporates
elements of European homes, which have
a small window in the roof (*dormer*), and
a balustrade (short fence that surrounded the terrace).
Roof forms are more similar to the roofs of Javanese
houses (*loji* – Western colonial style grand house).

*T*he entire wall of this house is layered with very beautiful wood.

The ornate glass and *art nouveau* style vent are also not to be missed.

Unfortunately, in the year 1997 this house did not escape from flooding that reached knee-height.

The homeowner, who can trace his lineage to the Han people, is very concerned about the condition of the house,

which could with the right maintenance become a protected cultural heritage site.

The P3GI Building
(Indonesian Sugar Research Institute)
– a historic icon of Pasuruan,
the world-renowned sugar town.
In this building, sugarcane seedlings were
processed to get the best seed.
Although times have changed, the workers
here should be respected for their dedication
in developing the country's food security.

Various buildings in Pasuruan, among others:
the train station, church, temple, and school buildings
from the era of Untung Suropati that was used
as a *Societeit* (club house) building,
a postcard with an image of Pasuruan in 1885,
proof of the fame and greatness of this city.

THE CENTER OF SUGAR

In the pre-colonial period, Surabaya was called Hujung Galuh. In the 11th century, Hujung Galuh began to develop and was an interinsular port, with many trading ships from the islands of Indonesia and abroad stopping to unload and load merchandise. According to the book notes of Ying Yai Sheng Lan (1416), Hujung Galuh was one of the three commercial port towns of Tuban, Gresik, and Surabaya.

As a busy port, Hujung Galuh was also a meeting place between nations. It was also stated that many rich people lived and resided in Surabaya, approximately 1,000 families, some of which were Tionghoa.

The decreasing influence of Majapahit in the 17th century was also marked by the decline of Hujung Galuh port (Surabaya). In this century, many people began arriving from Gujarat, Malabar, and Coromandel in South India to the coast of Gresik. In addition to trade, they also spread Islam. Apart from South India, many Muslim missionaries came from Hadramaut (the Hadrami). In Surabaya, they settled in and around Ampel.

Under an agreement dated 11 November 1743 between the Governor-General Baron van Imhoff with Pakubowono II, King of Mataram, full sovereignty over the city of Surabaya was handed over to the VOC. As sovereign, the VOC developed the downtown area (*kota bawah*) or *benedenstat* as a commercial center.

In accordance with *wijkenstelsel* regulations, in 1843 the downtown area of Surabaya was divided into two residential areas based on ethnic groups, namely

The construction of Jembatan Merah in the 19th century, the bridge that became a landmark of Surabaya (*right*).

The ground floor lobby of the PTPN XI (Persero) building, which is located on Jalan Merak, Surabaya, historical heritage which should be empowered (*left*).

The sura fish and the crocodile (*sura ing baya*) a symbol of the city of Surabaya, which means bravery in facing challenges (*previous page*).

the European settlement on the west side of *Jembatan Merah* and the foreign Eastern settlement (*Vreemde Oosterlingen*) on the East side, which consisted of the Tionghoa residential area (*Chineesche Kamp*), and the Arab residential area (*Arabische Kamp*). Bumiputera community settlements spread around the Tionghoa and Arab residential areas.

Rapid development occurred in the large cities of the Dutch East Indies, such as Surabaya, after the abolition of *cultuurstelsel* in 1870. That year is often regarded as the beginning of a new stage of development of the colonial era, where the cities grew rapidly in the presence of trade offices of Dutch companies, as in the city of Surabaya. One building that was the pride of Surabaya was the HVA building, which now functions as the PTPN XI (Persero) directors' office. HVA had in the Dutch era been the center of activity of the sugar industry. This beautiful and sturdy building was constructed in 1921 and until now is still maintained in its original form. A valuable architectural legacy that should be kept in existence.

Designed by Hulswit, Fermont and Ed Cuypers, a leading firm of architects and engineers in the Dutch East Indies from 1910 until 1942. The first and second floors of this building are circled by columned corridors, which have floral motifs forming Islamic writings. Its two-layered roof forms are a form of local expression as well as a solution to climate conditions.

Functional changes occurred in many areas around the PTPN XI (Persero) building. Some buildings were converted into warehouses, due to their concerning condition caused by the lack of maintenance and dull facades.

Surabaya City Government has made efforts to protect historic buildings through the decrees of the Mayor of Surabaya in 1996 and 1998, which stipulated about 163 buildings and sites that

The city of Surabaya has been the busy center of the sugar trade from the time of the Dutch East Indies until now, with a history that can be witnessed through the old colonial-style buildings.

should be protected. However, the efforts to protect the character of this area are not yet maximal. Cultural heritage conservation efforts should not only protect one or a few buildings, but should also maintain the city's structure (urban fabric), which includes land use patterns (functional buildings), architectural style, and the activities of community life that make the character of an area different and unique.

HVA At A Glance

Handelsvereeniging Amsterdam (HVA) was a private company founded in Amsterdam in 1879, shortly after the Cultivation System in the Dutch East Indies ended and the honeymoon phase of economic liberalization began. Initially, HVA was an agricultural bank (*cultuurbank*), which provided credit to plantation companies, crop exporters, and importers of plantation equipment and machinery. After the first world agricultural crisis in the 1880s, HVA became the owner of plantations in the Dutch East Indies by taking over the bankrupt debtors' properties. HVA began in 1910 to concentrate on the plantation business, and other businesses such as banking and importing plantation equipment. HVA established itself as the largest plantation company in the Dutch East Indies. The main commodity traded by HVA was sugar, concentrated in Java, as well as some other commodities such as rubber, coffee, tea, pepper, and pineapple fiber (*sisal*) in Sumatra. Apart from Amsterdam, HVA had offices in Surabaya and Medan.

During the Japanese occupation, almost all of HVA's business was frozen. It is recorded that only PG Djatiroto was allowed to operate to produce spirits and alcohol to meet the needs of Japan's war machine in World War II.

After Indonesia's independence, HVA and several other plantation companies, such as Internatio, Koloniale Bank, and others tried to recover their assets that had been taken by the Japanese army. Through the Linggardjati negotiation and the Round Table Conference (RTC), HVA managed to regain some of its assets, such as several sugar factories in Java and a tea plantation in Kajoe Aro Jambi, a palm plantation Bulu Blang Ara, and also the rubber plantation Aur Djambu, and Pulau Tiga, all in Aceh.

After all Dutch assets were nationalized in 1957, HVA was dissolved.

With its continuous development, Surabaya has become a very comfortable city that provides its residents with education and recreation. As a tourism destination, the city of Surabaya has very attractive potential to be developed.

Viewed from outside, this building already exudes charm. Moreover, once you set foot inside, the stained glass, golden ceramic walls, and HVA's vintage furniture really inspire awe in people who love old buildings.

*T*he HVA building
that currently serves as
the office of the PTPN XI
board of directors.
Built in 1921, the building
was designed by Hulswit,
Fermont and Ed Cuypers,
the largest architecture
and engineering firm
in the Dutch East Indies
community from
1910-1942.

*S*everal architectural details of the office building of PTPN XI (Persero) combine elements of local culture, and the building has become a source of pride to the city of Surabaya. The clock perched on the outside of the building is still active and referred to for information on local time. Ventilation and reliefs made of brass represent the image of luxury of the former HVA institution.

The tropical ambience of the office buildings of PTPN XI (Persero), formerly known as
the HVA building, can be detected not only from the roof, but also from the veranda.
The roof of the HVA building features a very local adaptation in the way that it channels the hot air
out of the building, while a veranda is a necessity in the tropics. Interestingly, the veranda of the HVA
building creates an effect that has the appearance of a roof composition supported by columns.

*B*uildings in the architectural style of eclecticism were constructed between the years 1910-1925.
The architect freely took decorative ornaments from local culture (Javanese and Western)
to create a very beautiful building.

*R*eliefs with the nuances of Javanese temples adorn the ressaut and ground floor *balustrade* surrounding this building. The *ressaut* is a prominent part of an architectural element. The *balustrade* is a ledge (hand rail) that surrounds a balcony or the top part (roof edge) of a building.

*I*ntricately detailed.
The textural lines on the columns
supporting the window are some
stylistic elements of the work of
architect Hulswit, Fermont and
Ed Cuypers, which combines
traditional and modern decoration,
especially Art Deco.

The main entrance to the lobby of the PTPN XI (Persero) building has a trellis decorated with a simple pattern of lines and mangosteen flower motifs, reminiscent of Balinese reliefs.

*T*he intricacies of the coffered ceiling and the minimalist lighting gives the impression of lightness to this combination of yellow walls and pillars of textured ceramic.

The team of maestro architects created works that are full of charm and absolutely unique. Ceramic reliefs of various types of commodity crops like rubber, coffee and others, surround the entire room above the lobby, while pillars are decorated with ornamental motifs of Hindu Java.

*A*t the end of the staircase handrail the mangosteen flower motif is an ornament
that we often see until today. The architect, who first came to the Dutch East Indies in 1906,
was attracted by this local decorative ornaments that later became his trademark.

The utmost appreciation should be given to the diligent maintenance of this property, which has meant that all furniture and furnishings can still be enjoyed today. Notice the antique lamps and chairs that fill this room.

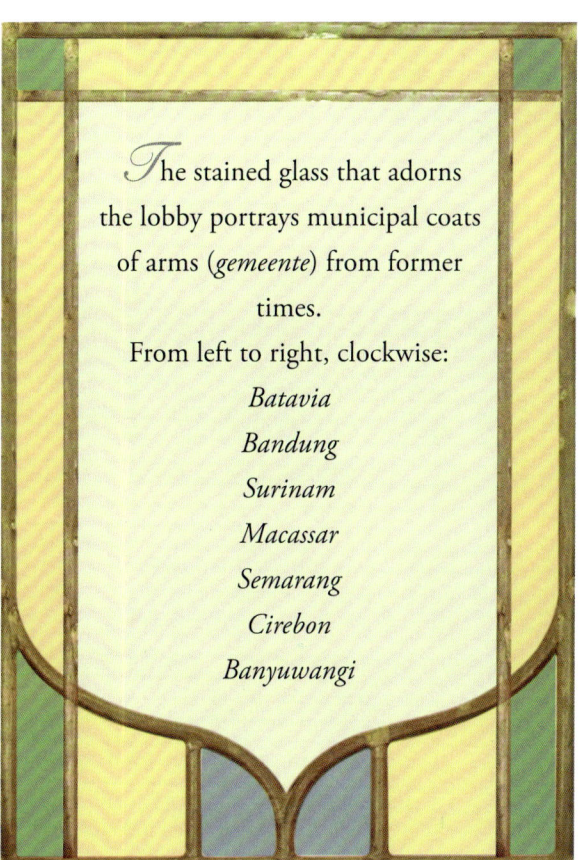

The stained glass that adorns the lobby portrays municipal coats of arms (*gemeente*) from former times.
From left to right, clockwise:

Batavia

Bandung

Surinam

Macassar

Semarang

Cirebon

Banyuwangi

The stained glass that surrounds the space is less complex in its design,
allowing the maximum amount of light to enter and beautify the lobby with its golden yellow nuance,
combining sweetly with the window shutters.

Office rooms supported by columns and partitioned by wood and glass.
Apart from not giving an overstated impression, it also makes the room more simple and elegant.
The panels are a new touch that do not disturb the harmonious unity of the interior.

*C*omfortable.

Although it doesn't have any cushions, this chair is very comfortable to sit in.

The proportion of the body and the inclination is well calculated.

The wood is always carefully selected. The older it is, the oilier;

without needing any special treatment, this chair is always shiny.

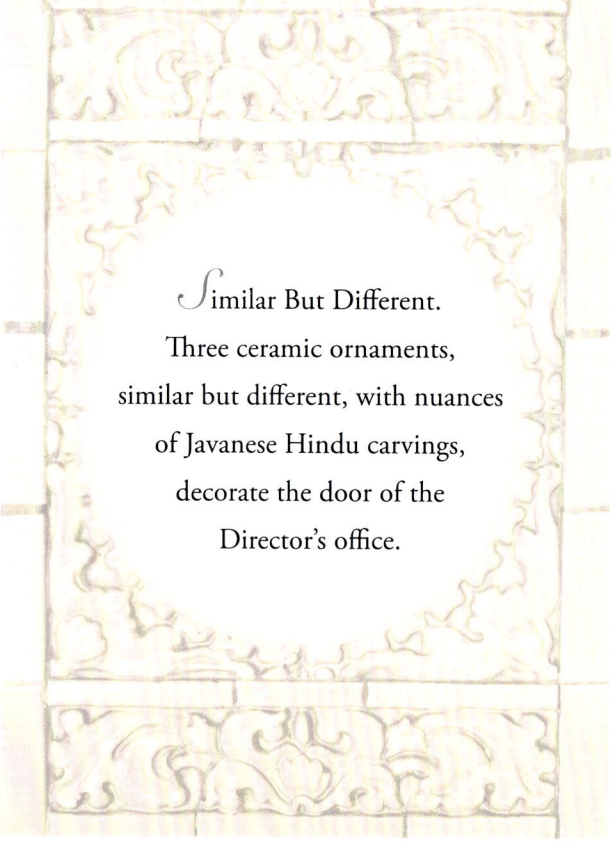

*S*imilar But Different.
Three ceramic ornaments,
similar but different, with nuances
of Javanese Hindu carvings,
decorate the door of the
Director's office.

The HVA building ceramic wall reliefs were made out of clay by the sculptor Jan Christofel Schulz, inspired by the paintings of WOJ Niewenkamp.

The final reliefs were made in the factory of *De Porceleyne Fles* in Delft in 1926.

*T*he coffered ceiling with its *tumpal batik* motifs on each side.
The architect seemed to always have a message to convey through highlighting
the cultural character of the decorative arts.

BIBLIOGRAPHY

Cahyono, Edi, *Karesidenan Pekalongan Kurun Cultuurstelsel: Masyarakat Pribumi Menyongsong Pabrik Gula*, Skripsi Sarjana S1, Jurusan Sejarah, Fakultas Sastra Universitas Indonesia, Juni 1988.

Djamhari, Saleh, A, **Strategi Menjinakkan Diponegoro (Stelsel Benteng 1827-1830)**, Jakarta :Yayasan Komunitas Bambu, 2004

Elson, Robert E., **Javanese Peasant and the Colonial Sugar Industry : Impact and Change in an East Java Residency**, 1830-1940, Singapore : Oxford University Press, 1984

Fasseur, Cornelis, **The Politics of Colonial Exploitattion, Java, the Dutch, and The Cultivation System** (terj RE Elson dan Ary Kraal), Ithaca, New York : Cornell Souheast Asian Program, 1994 (2nd printing).

Furnivall, J.S., **Hindia Belanda, Studi tentang Ekonomi Majemuk**, Jakarta : Freedom Institute, 2009

Haks, Leo and Guus Maris, **Lexicon of Foreign Artists who Visualized Indonesia 1600-1950)**, Singapore : Archipelago Press, 1995

Handinoto, *Sekilas Tentang Arsitektur Cina Pada Akhir Abad ke 19 di Pasuruan*, Dimensi,Volume 15, Juli 1990.

_____, *Perkembangan Bangunan Etnis Tionghoa di Indonesia. (akhir abad ke 19 sampai tahun 1960an)* (Artikel,tt)

_____, *Pasuruan dan Arsitektur Etnis China Akhir Abad 19 dan Awal Abad 20* (Makalah Simposium Arsitektur Vernakular 2, Pertemuan Arsitektur Nusantara, tt)

Heuken SJ, Adolf, **Sumber-sumber Asli Sejarah Jakarta, Jilid I, Dokumen-dokumen Sejarah Jakarta sampai dengan akhir abad ke-16**, Jakarta : Yayasan Cipta Loka Caraka, 1999

_____, **Sumber-sumber Asli Sejarah Jakarta Jilid II, Dokumen-dokumen Sejarah Jakarta dari Kedatangan kapal pertama Belanda (1596) sampai dengan tahun 1619)**, Jakarta : Yayasan Cipta Loka, 2000.

_____, **Sumber-sumber Asli Sejarah Jakarta Jilid III, Sumber-sumber sejarah pada dasawarsa pertama kota Batavia (1619-1630) dan kutipan dari karya sastra Indonesia yang menyangkut awal mula Jakarta**, Jakarta : Yayasan Cipta Loka Caraka, 2001.

Ishwara, Helen (ed.), **Pelangi Cina Indonesia**, Jakarta : Intisari Mediatama, 2002.

Knight, Roger G., *John Palmer and Plantation Development in Western Java During the Earlier Nineteenth Century*, Leiden : **Bijdragen tot de Taal, Land, en Volkenkunde** vol. 131, no. 203, 1975, hal. 307-309.

_____ and Arthur van Schalk, *State and Capital in Late Colonial Indonesia*, Leiden : **Bijdragen tot de**

Taal, Land en Volkenkunde, vol. 157, no.4, 2001, hal. 831-859.

Kunio, Yoshihara, *Oei Tiong Ham Concern : The First Business Empire of Southeast Asia*, **Southeast Asia Studies**, vol. 27, no. 2, September 1989, hal. 137-157

Khudori, **Gula Rasa Neoliberalisme, Pergumulan Empat Abad Industri Gula**, Jakarta : LP3ES, Jakarta, 2005.

Multatuli : **Max Havelar, Lelang Kopi Maskapai Dagang Belanda** (terj. HB Jassin), Jakarta : Djambatan, 2005 (cet. Ke 9)

Nn, *Sejarah Nusantara, (1602-1800)*, Wikipedia bahasa Indonesia, ensiklopedia bebas, tt

Puspitasari, Ika, Antariksa, Usman Fadly, **Pelestarian Kawasan Pecinan Kota Pasuruan**, Arsitektur e-Journal, Volume 2, Nomor 1, Maret 2009, hal. 21-33

P3GI, **Mengejar Sebuah Asa**, Pasuruan : P3GI, 2008.

Salmon, Claudine, *The Han family of East Java, Entrepreneurship and Politics (18th-19th Centuries)*, **Archipel**, vol. 41, numero 1, annee 1991, hal. 53-87

_____, *Some More Comments on "Uncertain Links" in the Han Lineage*, **Archipel**, vol. 62, numero 1, annee 2001, hal. 53-64.

_____, *The Han Family from the Residency of Besuki (East Java) as Reflected in a Novella by Tjoa Boen Sing (1910)*, **Archipel**, vol. 68, numero , annee 2004, hal 272-287.

Simbolon, Parakitri T., **Menjadi Indonesia, Buku I, Akar Akar Kebangsaan Indonesia**, Jakarta : Grasindo,1995.

Swantoro, P, **Dari Buku ke Buku, Sambung Menyambung Menjadi Satu**, Jakarta : Kepustakaan Populer Gramedia, 2002 (cet 2).

Tandjung, Krisnina Maharani, A., **Sekelumit Sejarah Mangkunegaran (1757- sekarang)**, Jakarta : Yayasan Warna Warni Indonesia, 2007

Tim Penulis PS, **Pembudidayaan Tebu di Lahan Sawah dan Tegalan**, Jakarta :Penebar Swadaya, 1995, cet. 2

Toer, Pramudya Ananta, **Jalan Raya Pos, Jalan Daendels**, Jakarta : Lentera Dipantara, 2005, cet.6

Wasino, **Kapitalisme Bumi Putera,Perubahan Masyarakat Mangkunegaran**, Yogyakarta :LKIS 2008, Jogjakarta.

Wijayati, Putri Agus, **Tanah dan Sistem Perpajakan Masa Kolonial Inggris**, Yogyakarta : Tarawang Press, 2001.

www.engefire.net/ale/aad/bantam1596

PHOTO LIST

Dok. **INDONESIA, Early 500 Postcards**, 159 (center)

Dok. **Lexicon Artist Who Visualized Indonesia** (1600-1950), 21, 22,103

Dok. **Rumah Abu Han Surabaya**, 102 (above left)

Dok **Yayasan Cipta Loka Caraka**, 20 (above)

Koleksi **KITLV**, 12,13,14,15,16-17, 23, 24, 25, 26, 27, 29, 30, 31, 32, 33, 34,

35, 36, 37, 38, 39 (above), 40, 41, 42, 43, 169, 171, 172 (above)

Koleksi **engelfriet.net** and **e-ducation.net**, 18, 19 (above left)

Koleksi **Tropenmuseum**, 39 (below)

WB Photography, all photos except listed above.

PRINSDOM

MADION

PANARAGA
Donborg

NARAGA

'T LANDSCHAP

CADIRIA
Caboul

'T LANDSCHAP

BRINDJOK

BRINDJOK

NIEUWE EN ZEER NAAUKEURIGE KAART
VAN T EYLAND
JAVA MAJOR
OF
GROOT JAVA
verdeeld in seven byzondere bestekken
door FRANÇOIS VALENTYN. V.D.M.